MW01268235

The Creed of the Old South
1865-1915

BY
Basil L. Gildersleeve

Civil War Classic Library

PREFACE

In the last score of years I have often been urged by friends and sympathizers to bring out as a separate issue my article, The Creed of the Old South, which appeared in the Atlantic Monthly of January, 1892, and which attracted wider attention than anything I have ever written. As this is the jubilee of the great year 1865, the memories of that distant time come thronging back to the actors in the momentous struggle, and I am prompted to publish in more accessible form my record of views and impressions that may seem strange even to the survivors of the conflict, now rapidly passing away. To this paper I have added an essay on a cognate theme--A Southerner in the Peloponnesian War--which was published in the Atlantic Monthly of September, 1897, and which has been accepted by the eminent historian, Mr. Rhodes, as an historical document. These specimens of what I call my Sargasso work ("Weeds from the Atlantic") are reproduced by the kind permission of the Houghton Mifflin Company. A few slips of pen and type have been corrected, and a few notes out of the mass of literature evoked by the first essay, or akin to it, have been added for the benefit of the third generation.

THE JOHNS HOPKINS UNIVERSITY,   JUNE,
1915.

Civil War Classic Library

THE CREED OF THE OLD SOUTH

[Note: This article was prepared (in 1891) at the instance of Mr. HORACE SCUDDER, the editor of the Atlantic Monthly, who had projected a series of papers to be written by men who by virtue of education, intellectual endowment and social position were supposed to be high and lifted up above vulgar passion and prejudice. The business of these elect gentlemen was to set forth the motives that urged them to an active participation in so rude an affair as war. After publication in the Atlantic, the essays were to be gathered into a book and Mr. SCUDDER fancied that thus collected they would prove a valuable addition to the history of the times. The series stopped at the third number and the book was never published. Whilst I did not concur in Mr. SCUDDER'S view, I accepted the compliment and began to write with a lighter heart than I bore as I went on. At the end I was dipping my pen into something red, into something briny, that was not ink. The feeling seems to have been contagious, for some years afterwards (1899) Mr. WILLIAM ARCHER, in his America To-day (p. 142), wrote as follows:

"I met a scholar-soldier in the South who had given expression to the sentiment of his race and generation in an essay--one might almost say an elegy--so chivalrous in spirit and so fine in literary form that it moved me well-nigh to tears. Reading it at a public library, I found myself so visibly affected by it that my neighbor at the desk glanced at me in surprise, and I had to pull myself sharply together."]

A few months ago, as I was leaving Baltimore for a summer sojourn on the coast of Maine, two old soldiers of the war between the States took their seats immediately behind me in the car, and began a lively conversation about the various battles in which they had faced each other more than a quarter of a century ago, when a trip to New England would have been no holiday jaunt for one of their fellow-travellers. The veterans went into the minute detail that always puts me to shame, when I think how poor an account I should give, if pressed to describe the military movements that I have happened to witness; and I may as well acknowledge at the outset that I have as little aptitude for the soldier's trade as I have for the romancer's. Single incidents I remember as if they were of yesterday. Single pictures have burned themselves into my brain. But I have no vocation to tell how fields were lost and won; and my experience of military life was too brief and desultory to be of any value to the historian of the war. For my own life that experience has been of the utmost significance, and despite the heavy price I have had to pay for my outings, despite the daily reminder of five long months of intense suffering, I have no regrets. An able-bodied young man, with a long vacation at his disposal, could not have done otherwise, and the right to teach Southern youth for nine months was earned by sharing the fortunes of their fathers and brothers at the front for three. Self-respect is everything; and it is something to have belonged in deed and in truth to an heroic generation, to have shared in a measure its perils and privations. But that heroic generation is apt to be a bore to a generation whose heroism is of a different type, and I doubt whether the young people in our car took much interest in the very audible conversation of the two veterans. Twenty-five years hence, when the survivors will be curiosities, as were Revolutionary pensioners in my childhood, there may be a renewal of interest. As it is, few of the present generation pore over The Battles and Leaders of the Civil War, and a grizzled old Confederate has been heard to declare that he intended to bequeath his copy of that valuable work to some one outside of the family, so provoked was he at the supineness of his children. And yet, for the truth's sake, all these battles must be fought over and over again, until the account is cleared, and until justice is done to the valor and skill of both sides.

[Note: I had a similar experience some years after I wrote this paper, when I was spending the summer at Westport on Lake Champlain. Wandering far enough off into the country to lose myself--for me no unfamiliar feat--I joined a man who was driving his cows to town and in my talk with him it turned out that he had been through the Valley campaign on the other side, and together we recalled encounters and scenes that were not recorded in the histories, insignificant skirmishes-- significant enough to those who were killed and maimed. Who remembers the little brush at Weyer's Cave, where the Confederates came near bagging General Merritt? I have not been allowed to forget it these fifty years.]

The two old soldiers were talking amicably enough, as all old soldiers do, but they "yarned," as all old soldiers do, and though they talked from Baltimore to Philadelphia, and from Philadelphia to New York, their conversation was lost on me, for my thoughts went back into my own past, and two pictures came up to me from the time of the war.

[Note: Apropos of this passage my friend and classmate of the Princeton days, Gen. BRADLEY T. JOHNSON, told me that one hot day riding to meet a fight that would make the day still hotter, he stopped at a roadside cabin and asked for a drink of water. The woman who brought it, brought it in a broken and cracked mug, and he assured me that every ramification of those cracks was indelibly impressed on his brain. He could have drawn a map of the mug. Experiences like these help us to understand the details of the Homeric narrative, and to me there is nothing unnatural in Homer's mention of the washing troughs that Hector saw as he fled before the face of Achilles (Il. 22, 154 foll.).]

Civil War Classic Library

[Note: The fight under EARLY, to which I refer, was fought July 24, 1864. It was a brilliant feat of arms and has left other memories than those recorded. As A. D. C. to General GORDON I gave General TERRY, one of the brigade commanders, the order to advance, and I still hear the cry of one of the men who had been in a disastrous affair a few weeks before--the fight in which Gen. W. E. JONES fell. "This hain't no New Hope, Gineral." I still see the light of battle on the faces of the men as they went forward. My blood tingles as I write.]

In the midsummer of 1863 I was serving as a private in the First Virginia Cavalry. Gettysburg was in the past, and there was not much fighting to be done, but the cavalry was not wholly idle. Raids had to be intercepted, and the enemy was not to be allowed to vaunt himself too much; so that I gained some experience of the hardships of that arm of the service, and found out by practical participation what is meant by a cavalry charge. To a looker-on nothing can be finer. To the one who charges, or is supposed to charge,--for the horse seemed to me mainly responsible,--the details are somewhat cumbrous. Now in one of these charges some of us captured a number of the opposing force, among them a young lieutenant. Why this particular capture should have impressed me so I cannot tell, but memory is a tricky thing. A large red fox scared up from his lair by the fight at Castleman's Ferry stood for a moment looking at me; and I shall never forget the stare of that red fox. At one of our fights near Kernstown a spent bullet struck a horse on the side of his nose, which happened to be white, and left a perfect imprint of itself; and the jerk of the horse's head and the outline of the bullet are present to me still. The explosion of a particular caisson, the shriek of a special shell, will ring in one's ears for life. A captured lieutenant was no novelty, and yet this captured lieutenant caught my eye and held it. A handsomer young fellow, a more noble-looking, I never beheld

among Federals or Confederates, as he stood
there, bare-headed, among his captors, erect
and silent. His eyes were full of fire, his
lips showed a slight quiver of scorn, and his
hair seemed to tighten its curls in defiance.
Doubtless I had seen as fine specimens of young
manhood before, but if so, I had seen without
looking, and this man was evidently what we
called a gentleman.

[Note: "Deboshed" is a reminiscence of an essay
of LOWELL'S on Reconstruction, in which he
makes light of Southern claims to aristocracy.]

Southern men were proud of being gentlemen,
although they have been told in every
conceivable tone that it was a foolish pride,--
foolish in itself, foolish in that it did not
have the heraldic backing that was claimed for
it; the utmost concession being that a number
of "deboshed" younger sons of decayed gentry
had been shipped to Virginia in the early
settlement of that colony. But the very pride
played its part in making us what we were proud
of being, and whether descendants of the
aforesaid "deboshed," of simple English yeomen,
of plain Scotch-Irish Presbyterians, a sturdy
stock, of Huguenots of various ranks of life,
we all held to the same standard, and showed,
as was thought, undue exclusiveness on this
subject. But this prisoner was the embodiment
of the best type of Northern youth, with a
spirit as high, as resolute, as could be found
in the ranks of Southern gentlemen; and though
in theory all enlightened Southerners
recognized the high qualities of some of our
opponents, this one noble figure in "flesh and
blood" was better calculated to inspire respect
for "those people," as we had learned to call
our adversaries, than many pages of "gray
theory."

[Note: General LEE always referred to the enemy
as "those people." JOHN S. WISE, Atlantic
Monthly, April, 1894. WISE is one ear-witness
among many, and I thought of General LEE, as

well as of Dante, when I wrote in my Introductory Essay to Pindar, xxxviii:

A word, an epithet, and the picture is there, drawn with a stroke. In the second Olympian P. is telling of the blessedness of the souls that have overcome. When he comes to the damned, he calls them simply "those."--_Non ragioniam di lor._]

[Note: Lieut. Gen. JOHN B. GORDON, Reminiscences, p. 422. Perhaps I may be pardoned for adding that when I read the passage in which mention is made of my service on his staff, I wrote to my chief, whose own bearing on the battlefield was an inspiration, that no tribute to my Greek scholarship I had received or could receive would ever be more cherished, if so much; and I cited the famous epitaph inscribed on the tomb of Aeschylus at Gela. No mention is made of his great tragedies. It is simply recorded that Aeschylus had quitted himself like a man in the Persian war.

[Greek: alkên d' eudokimon Marathônion alsos an eipoi kai bathychaitêeis Mêdos epistamenos.]

In these Notes I am furnishing a key to the persons referred to in the article. There is a Confederate graveyard near my old home, the University of Virginia, in which hundreds of those who fell on the field or perished in the hospital, were laid to rest. At first a rude headboard marked each grave with the name, the company, the regiment, to be replaced, it was thought, by some more substantial monument at the end of the war; but the end of the war brought the consciousness of dire poverty that could hardly furnish food for the living, and so it was sadly resolved rather than leave these ghastly and decaying reminders of individual suffering and sacrifice to level the whole field and sow it in grass, but not until a pious soul, an English artist who bore the

un-English name of SCHARF, had recorded each
name and the place of burial on an elaborate
plat. Still I cannot forbear to contribute my
rude shingle here and there to the memory of my
comrades. The staff-officer mentioned here was
GEORGE H. WILLIAMSON, of Maryland. Two years
before I made his acquaintance Mr. _William M.
Blackford_, of Lynchburg, wrote in his diary,
since privately printed, under the date July
25, 1862: Williamson, an interesting man,
educated at Harvard and abroad, was a rising
lawyer in Baltimore when the war broke out and
he enlisted as a private in a Maryland
regiment.]

[Note: A revival of religion to counterbalance,
as it were, the revival of brutality, is a
recurring phenomenon of great wars. The tide of
skepticism in Greece was checked by the Persian
War, and even to-day the French army shews a
return to the Man of Sorrows, whose effigy had
been removed from all public buildings.]

A little more than a year afterwards, in
Early's Valley campaign,--a rude school of
warfare,--I was serving as a volunteer aide on
General Gordon's staff. The day before the
disaster of Fisher's Hill I was ordered,
together with another staff officer, to
accompany the general on a ride to the front.
The general had a well-known weakness for
inspecting the outposts,--a weakness that made
a position in his suite somewhat precarious.
The officer with whom I was riding had not been
with us long, and when he joined the staff had
just recovered from wounds and imprisonment. A
man of winning appearance, sweet temper, and
attractive manners, he soon made friends of the
military family, and I never learned to love a
man so much in so brief an acquaintance, though
hearts knit quickly in the stress of war. He
was highly educated, and foreign residence and
travel had widened his vision without affecting
the simple faith and thorough consecration of
the Christian. Here let me say that the bearing
of the Confederates is not to be understood
without taking into account the deep religious

feeling of the army and its great leaders. It is an historical element, like any other, and is not to be passed over in summing up the forces of the conflict. "A soldier without religion," says a Prussian officer, who knew our army as well as the German, "is an instrument without value"; and it is not unlikely that the knowledge of the part that faith played in sustaining the Southern people may have lent emphasis to the expression of his conviction.

We rode together towards the front, and as we rode our talk fell on Goethe and on Faust, and of all passages the soldiers' song came up to my lips,--the song of soldiers of fortune, not the chant of men whose business it was to defend their country. Two lines, however, were significant:--

      Kühn ist das Mühen,   Herrlich der Lohn.

We reached the front. An occasional "zip" gave warning that the sharpshooters were not asleep, and the quick eye of the general saw that our line needed rectification and how. Brief orders were given to the officer in command. My comrade was left to aid in carrying them out. The rest of us withdrew. Scarcely had we ridden a hundred yards towards camp when a shout was heard, and, turning round, we saw one of the men running after us. "The captain had been killed." The peace of heaven was on his face, as I gazed on the noble features that afternoon. The bullet had passed through his official papers and found his heart. He had received his discharge, and the glorious reward had been won.

This is the other picture that the talk of the two old soldiers called up,--dead Confederate against living Federal; and these two pictures stand out before me again, as I am trying to make others understand and to understand myself what it was to be a Southern man twenty-five years ago; what it was to accept with the whole heart the creed of the Old South. The image of the living Federal bids me refrain from harsh words in the presence of those who were my captors. The dead Confederate bids me uncover the sacred memories that the dust of life's Appian Way hides from the tenderest and truest of those whose business it is to live and work. For my dead comrade of the Valley campaign is one of many; some of them my friends, some of them my pupils as well. The 18th of July, 1861, laid low one of my Princeton College room-mates; on the 21st, the day of the great battle, the other fell,--both bearers of historic names, both upholding the cause of their State with as unclouded a conscience as any saint in the martyrology ever wore; and from that day to the end, great battle and outpost skirmish brought me, week by week, a personal loss in men of the same type.

[Note: The Princeton College room-mate who fell on the 18th of July was JAMES KENDALL LEE, a distant relative of the great soldier; the other was PEYTON RANDOLPH HARRISON, of Martinsburg (W.) Va., representative of the oldest families in the old state. His brother, DABNEY CARR HARRISON (Princeton, '48), another close friend, took service in the Confederate army, first as chaplain, then as captain of a company, and was killed at Fort Donelson which, as I painfully remember, was at first reported as a Confederate victory.]

The surrender of the Spartans on the island of Sphacteria was a surprise to friend and foe alike; and the severe historian of the Peloponnesian war pauses to record the answer of a Spartan to the jeering question of one of the allies of the Athenians,--a question which implied that the only brave Spartans were those who had been slain. The answer was tipped with Spartan wit; the only thing Spartan, as some one has said, in the whole un-Spartan affair. "The arrow," said he, "would be of great price if it distinguished the brave men from the cowards." But it did seem to us, in our passionate grief, that the remorseless bullet, the remorseless shell, had picked out the bravest and the purest. It is an old cry,--

Ja, der Krieg verschlingt die Besten.

Still, when Schiller says in the poem just quoted,

Ohne Wahl vertheilt die Gaben,   Ohne Billigkeit das Glück,   Denn Patroklus liegt begraben   Und Thersites kommt zurück,

his illustration is only half right. The Greek Thersites did not return to claim a pension.

[Note: Thersites--strange that Schiller in his Siegeslied should have forgotten it--never lived to return. According to the Scholia Vetera on Lycophron, 999, this monkey-shaped ([Greek: pithêkomorphos]) creature was slain by Achilles for gouging out the eyes of Penthesilea's maid, with whom Achilles had fallen in love. A better point was made by Ovid, that master of points (Am. 2, 6, 41): _Tristia Phylacidae Thersites funera vidit._]

[Note: The French artist was GUILLAUME, who came to this country shortly before the war. In the picture to which I refer, General LEE was the main figure. GUILLAUME'S picture of the Surrender at Appomattox bore evidence of minute study of every detail of that historic event.]

Of course, what was to all true Confederates beyond a question "a holy cause," "the holiest of causes," this fight in defence of "the sacred soil" of our native land, was to the other side "a wicked rebellion" and "damnable treason," and both parties to the quarrel were not sparing of epithets which, at this distance of time, may seem to our children unnecessarily

undignified; and no doubt some of these
epitheta ornantia continue to flourish in
remote regions, just as pictorial
representations of Yankees and rebels in all
their respective fiendishness are still
cherished here and there. At the Centennial
Exposition of 1876, by way of conciliating the
sections, the place of honour in the "Art
Annex," was given to Rothermel's painting of
the battle of Gettysburg, in which the face of
every dying Union soldier is lighted up with a
celestial smile, while guilt and despair are
stamped on the wan countenances of the moribund
rebels. At least such is my recollection of the
painting; and I hope that I may be pardoned for
the malicious pleasure I felt when I was
informed of the high price that the State of
Pennsylvania had paid for that work of art. The
dominant feeling was amusement, not
indignation. But as I looked at it I recalled
another picture of a battle-scene, painted by a
friend of mine, a French artist, who had
watched our life with an artist's eye. One of
the figures in the foreground was a dead
Confederate boy, lying in the angle of a worm
fence. His uniform was worn and ragged, mud-
stained as well as blood-stained; the cap which
had fallen from his head was a tatter, and the
torn shoes were ready to drop from his
stiffening feet; but in a buttonhole of his
tunic was stuck the inevitable toothbrush,
which continued even to the end of the war to
be the distinguishing mark of gentle nurture,--
the souvenir that the Confederate so often
received from fair sympathizers in border
towns. I am not a realist, but I would not
exchange that homely toothbrush in the
Confederate's buttonhole for the most angelic
smile that Rothermel's brush could have
conjured up.

[Note: The toothbrush was a badge of culture on
both sides, as the following passage shows:

"'Light marching order' implies that a soldier
may carry upon his person only a few of the
more obvious necessities of life and no

luxuries save tobacco. But a soldier must be clad even to sixty rounds of ball cartridge. Small wonder is it then, if only the lightest toothbrush drawn through the buttonhole of his blouse must suffice as an epitome of the refinements of life. Many of the victories of our adversaries were fairly attributed to the scantier attire and lighter marching order of the men."--Atlantic Monthly, May, 1893, p. 214.]

[Note: DAVID RAMSAY, grandson of the historian and biographer of Washington of the same name, my fellow-student at Göttingen in 1852, fell after heroic services at Battery Wagner in 1863. What the state, what the country lost in the promise of that rare man, this is not the place to rehearse. Scholar, wit, embodiment of all the inherited social graces of what we once called "the better days," delightful companion, devoted and generous friend, he is still in memory part of my life.]

Now I make no doubt that most of the readers of The Atlantic have got beyond the Rothermel stage, and yet I am not certain that all of them appreciate the entire clearness of conscience with which we of the South went into the war. A new patriotism is one of the results of the great conflict, and the power of local patriotism is no longer felt to the same degree. In one of his recent deliverances Mr. Carnegie, a canny Scot who has constituted himself the representative of American patriotism, says, "The citizen of the republic to-day is prouder of being an American than he is of being a native of any State in the country." What it is to be a native of any State in the country, especially an old State with an ancient and honorable history, is something that Mr. Carnegie cannot possibly understand. But the "to-day" is superfluous. The Union was a word of power in 1861 as it is in 1891. Before the secession of Virginia a Virginian Breckinridge asked: "If exiled in a foreign land, would the heart turn back to Virginia, or South Carolina, or New York, or to any one State as the cherished home of its pride? No. We would remember only that we were Americans." Surely this seems quite as patriotic as Mr. Carnegie's utterance; and yet, to the native Virginian just quoted, so much stronger was the State than the central government that, a few weeks after this bold speech, he went into the war, and finally perished in the war. "A Union man," says his biographer, "fighting for the rights of his old mother, Virginia." And there were many men of his mind, noted generals, valiant soldiers. The University Memorial, which records the names and lives of the alumni of the University of Virginia who fell in the Confederate war, two hundred in number,--this volume, full "of memories and of sighs" to every Southern man of my age, lies open before me as I write, and some of the noblest men who figure in its pages were Union men; and the Memorial of the Virginia Military Institute tells the same story with the same eloquence. The State was imperilled, and parties disappeared; and of the combatants in the field, some of the bravest and the most conspicuous belonged to those whose love of the old Union was warm and strong, to whom the severance of the tie that bound the States together was a personal grief. But even those who prophesied the worst, who predicted a long and bloody struggle and a doubtful result, had no question about the duty of the citizen; shared the common burden and submitted to the individual sacrifice as readily as the veriest fire-eater,--nay, as they claimed, more readily. The most intimate friend I ever had, who fell after heroic services, was known by all our circle to be utterly at variance with the prevalent Southern view of the quarrel, and died upholding a right which was not a right to him except so far as the mandate of his State made it a right; and while he would have preferred to see "the old flag" floating over a united people, he restored the new banner to its place time after time when it had been cut down by shot and shell.

[Note: For Pericles' budget, see Thuc. 2, 13.

Thuc. 1, 141: [Greek: tên autên dynatai doulôsin hê te megistê kai elachistê dikaiôsis apo tôn homoiôn pro dikês tois pelas epitassomenê.]]

Those who were bred in the opposite political faith, who read their right of withdrawal in the Constitution, had less heart-searching to begin with than the Union men of the South; but when the State called there were no parties, and the only trace of the old difference was a certain rivalry which should do the better fighting. This ready response to the call of the State showed very clearly that, despite varying theories of government, the people of the Southern States were practically of one mind as to the seat of the paramount obligation. Adherence to the Union was a matter of sentiment, a matter of interest. The arguments urged on the South against secession were addressed to the memories of the glorious struggle for independence, to the anticipation of the glorious future that awaited the united country, to the difficulties and the burdens of a separate life. Especial stress was laid on the last argument; and the expense of a separate government, of a standing army, was set forth in appalling figures. A Northern student of the war once said to me, "If the Southern people had been of a statistical turn, there would have been no secession, there would have been no war." But there were men enough of a statistical turn in the South to warn the people against the enormous expense of independence, just as there are men enough of a statistical turn in Italy to remind the Italians of the enormous cost of national unity. "Counting the cost" is in things temporal the only wise course, as in the building of a tower; but there are times in the life of an individual, of a people, when the things that are eternal force themselves into the calculation, and the abacus is nowhere. "Neither count I my life dear unto myself" is a sentiment that does not enter into the domain of statistics. The great Athenian statesman who saw the necessity of the Peloponnesian war was not above statistics, as he showed when he passed in review the resources of the Athenian empire, the tribute from the allies, the treasure laid up in the House of the Virgin. But when he addressed the people in justification of the war, he based his argument, not on a calculation of material resources, but on a simple principle of right. Submission to any encroachment, the least as well as the greatest, on the rights of a State means slavery. To us submission meant slavery, as it did to Pericles and the Athenians; as it did to the great historian of Greece, who had learned this lesson from the Peloponnesian war, and who took sides with the Southern States, to the great dismay of his fellow-radicals, who could not see, as George Grote saw, the real point at issue in the controversy. Submission is slavery, and the bitterest taunt in the vocabulary of those who advocated secession was "submissionist." But where does submission begin? Who is to mark the point of encroachment? That is a matter which must be decided by the sovereign; and on the theory that the States are sovereign, each State must be the judge. The extreme Southern States considered their rights menaced by the issue of the presidential election. Virginia and the Border States were more deliberate; and Virginia's "pausing" was the theme of much mockery in the State and out of it, from friend and from foe alike. Her love of peace, her love of the Union, were set down now to cowardice, now to cunning. The Mother of States and Queller of Tyrants was caricatured as Mrs. Facing-both-ways; and the great commonwealth that even Mr. Lodge's statistics cannot displace from her leadership in the history of the country was charged with trading on her neutrality. Her solemn protest was unheeded. The "serried phalanx of her gallant sons" that should "prevent the passage of the United States forces" was an expression that amused Northern critics of style as a bit of antiquated Southern rodomontade. But the call for troops showed that the rodomontade meant something. Virginia had made her decision; and if the United States forces did not find a serried phalanx barring their way,--a serried phalanx is somewhat out of date,--they found something that answered the purpose as well.

[Note: The friend was the late A. MARSHALL ELLIOTT, Professor of Romance Languages in the Johns Hopkins, whose life of study was matched by a life of adventure.]

The war began, the war went on. Passion was roused to fever heat. Both sides "saw red," that physiological condition which to a Frenchman excuses everything. The proverbial good humor of the American people did not, it is true, desert the country, and the Southern men who were in the field, as they were much happier than those who stayed at home, if I may judge by my own experience, were often merry enough by the camp fire, and exchanged rough jests with the enemy's pickets. But the invaded people were very much in earnest, however lightly some of their adversaries treated the matter, and as the pressure of the war grew tighter the more sombre did life become. A friend of mine, describing the crowd that besieged the Gare de Lyon in Paris, when the circle of fire was drawing round the city, and foreigners were hastening to escape, told me that the press was so great that he could touch in every direction those who had been crushed to death as they stood, and had not had room to fall. Not wholly unlike this was the pressure brought to bear on the Confederacy. It was only necessary to put out your hand and you touched a corpse; and that not an alien corpse, but the corpse of a brother or a friend. Every Southern man becomes grave when he thinks of that terrible stretch of time, partly, it is true, because life was nobler, but chiefly because of the memories of sorrow and suffering. A professional Southern humorist once undertook to write in dialect a Comic History of the War, but his heart failed him, as his public would have failed him, and the serial lived only for a number or two.

[Note: Those who suffered in Sherman's March to the Sea--I was riveted to my bed at the time--were not, are not so philosophic. See the narrative in BRADLEY JOHNSON'S Life of Joseph E. Johnston. Nor was I so philosophical when I followed the raiders of 1863, nor when I saw the fires that lighted up the Valley of Virginia in 1864, and that was before the systematic devastation recorded by MERRITT, who carried it out. "When our army," says MERRITT (Battles and Leaders, 4, 512), "commenced its return march, the cavalry was deployed across the Valley, burning, destroying or taking nearly everything of value, or likely to be of value to the enemy. It was a severe measure, and appears severer now in the lapse of time, but it was necessary as a measure of war." The plea of 1864 was the same as the plea of 1914. In a vivid sketch of Sherman's March, Prof. HENRY E. SHEPHERD, whose North Carolina home, Fayetteville, lay in the track of the invaders (Battles and Leaders, 4, 678) winds up by saying that the portrayal of it "baffles all the resources of literary art and the affluence even of our English speech," and those who know Professor SHEPHERD'S resources and affluence will recognize the desperate nature of the task. As for the Valley, I have before me a protest against the erection of a monument to Sheridan, in which the writer gives an itemized account of the havoc inflicted on the property of non-combatants in the County of Rockingham alone. The protest reminds me of my youthful surprise when I first saw the statue of Tilly in the Feldherrnhalle at Munich. Somehow I had not thought well of Tilly before. But all estimates of military exigencies must be revised by the light of the new standards of the time in which we live. However, as this note goes to the printer, I am made aware of an article by Maj. JOHN BIGELOW, U. S. A., published in the N. Y. Times of June 13, 1915, in which the author musters the evidence of the

behaviour of Sherman's men. 1864 seems not to
have been so very far behind 1914 after all.]

[Note: "The hate of Celt to Saxon, and the
contempt of Saxon for Celt, simply paled and
grew expressionless when compared with the
contempt and hate felt by the Southron towards
the Yankee anterior to our Civil War and while
it was in progress. No Houyhnhnms ever looked
on Yahoo with greater aversion; better, far
better death than further contamination through
political association."--C. F. ADAMS, Trans-
Atlantic Historical Solidarity, p. 176.

One recalls Halleck's Connecticut:

                    Virginians look   Upon them
with as favorable eyes   As Gabriel on the
devil in paradise.]

The war began, the war went on. War is a rough
game. It is an omelet that cannot be made
without breaking eggs, not only eggs in _esse_,
but also eggs in _posse_. So far as I have read
about war, ours was no worse than some other
wars. While it lasted, the conduct of the
combatants on either side was represented in
the blackest colors by the other. Even the
ordinary and legitimate doing to death was
considered criminal if the deed was done by a
ruthless rebel or a ruffianly invader. Non-
combatants were especially eloquent. In
describing the end of a brother who had been
killed while trying to get a shot at a Yankee,
a Southern girl raved about the "murdered
patriot" and the "dastardly wretch" who had
anticipated him. But I do not criticize, for I
remember an English account of the battle of
New Orleans, in which General Pakenham was
represented as having been picked off by a
"sneaking Yankee rifle." Those who were engaged
in the actual conflict took more reasonable
views, and the annals of the war are full of
stories of battlefield and hospital in which a
common humanity asserted itself. But

brotherhood there was none. No alienation could have been more complete. Into the cleft made by the disruption poured all the bad blood that had been breeding from colonial times, from Revolutionary times, from constitutional struggles, from congressional debates, from "bleeding Kansas" and the engine-house at Harper's Ferry; and a great gulf was fixed, as it seemed forever, between North and South. The hostility was a very satisfactory one--for military purposes.

[Note: Needless to say, the conspiracy theory has long been discarded. Mr. PAXSON, Professor of American History in the University of Wisconsin, has devoted a volume to shew that while the South was defending an impossible cause, it could not hold different views--that these were the unavoidable result of environment and natural resources. How different is all this from what the N. Y. Times lately reprinted from its issue of April 17, 1865.

"Every possible atrocity appertains to this rebellion. There is nothing whatever that its leaders have scrupled at. Wholesale massacres and torturings, wholesale starvation of prisoners, firing of great cities, piracies of the cruelest kind, persecution of the most hideous character and of vast extent, and finally assassination in high places--whatever is inhuman, whatever is brutal, whatever is fiendish, these men have resorted to. They will leave behind names so black, and the memory of deeds so infamous, that the execration of the slaveholders' rebellion will be eternal."

True, "slaveholders' rebellion" still survives here and there. So WILLIAM HARRISON CLARKE, in The Civil Service Law, Preface, says:

"Parties, when they strive solely for principle, are the life of a nation; but when they strive solely for pelf, patronage, and power they are its death. Even corrupt party leaders may destroy a republic; sometimes even ambitious leaders may do so. Did a nation ever make a narrower escape than did our own during the slaveholders' rebellion? Who but ambitious party leaders caused that rebellion?"]

[Note: "Vous êtes de France, mais je suis de Bretagne." "Eh bien! Ce n'est pas le même pays." "Mais c'est la même patrie." La femme se borna à répondre, "Je suis de Siscoingnard."-- V. HUGO, Quatre-Vingt-Treize.]

The war began, the war went on,--this politicians' conspiracy, this slaveholders' rebellion, as it was variously called by those who sought its source, now in the disappointed ambition of the Southern leaders, now in the desperate determination of a slaveholding oligarchy to perpetuate their power, and to secure forever their proprietorship in their "human chattels." On this theory the mass of Southern people were but puppets in the hands of political wirepullers, or blind followers of hectoring "patricians." To those who know the Southern people nothing can be more absurd; to those who know their personal independence, to those who know the deep interest which they have always taken in politics, the keen intelligence with which they have always followed the questions of the day. The court-house green was the political university of the Southern masses, and the hustings the professorial chair, from which the great political and economical questions of the day were presented, to say the least, as fully and intelligently as in the newspapers to which so much enlightenment is attributed. There was no such system of rotten boroughs, no such domination of a landed aristocracy, throughout the South as has been imagined, and venality, which is the disgrace of current politics, was practically unknown. The men who represented the Southern people in Washington came from the people, and not from a ring. Northern writers who have ascribed the firm control in Congress of the national government which the South held so long to the superior character, ability, and experience of its representatives, do not seem

24

to be aware that the choice of such representatives and their prolonged tenure show that in politics, at least, the education of the Southerner had not been neglected. The rank and file then were not swayed simply by blind passion or duped by the representations of political gamesters. Nor did the lump need the leavening of the large percentage of men of the upper classes who served as privates, some of them from the beginning to the end of the war. The rank and file were, to begin with, in full accord with the great principles of the war, and were sustained by the abiding conviction of the justice of the cause. Of course, there were in the Southern army, as in every army, many who went with the multitude in the first enthusiastic rush, or who were brought into the ranks by the needful process of conscription; but it is not a little remarkable that few of the poorest and the most ignorant could be induced to forswear the cause and to purchase release from the sufferings of imprisonment by the simple process of taking the oath. Those who have seen the light of battle on the faces of these humble sons of the South, or witnessed their steadfastness in camp, on the march, in the hospital, have not been ashamed of the brotherhood.

There is such a thing as fighting for a principle, an idea; but principle and idea must be incarnate, and the principle of States' rights was incarnate in the historical life of the Southern people. Of the thirteen original States, Virginia, North Carolina, South Carolina, and Georgia were openly and officially upon the side of the South. Maryland as a State was bound hand and foot. We counted her as ours, for the Potomac and Chesapeake Bay united as well as divided. Each of these States had a history, had an individuality. Every one was something more than a certain aggregate of square miles wherein dwelt an uncertain number of uncertain inhabitants, something more than a Territory transformed into a State by the magic of political legerdemain; a creature of the

central government, and duly loyal to its
creator.

[Note: "The brandished sword of her coat of
arms would have shown what manner of _placida
quies_ she would have ensued." The proof-reader
of the Atlantic not being over-familiar with
the Massachusetts coat of arms (_Ense petit
placidam sub libertate quietem_) or Scriptural
language, substituted for the foregoing what
one reads in the article as printed in the
Atlantic (p. 82): "The brandished sword would
have shown what manner of _placida quies_ would
have ensued...."]

[Note: The wish that South Carolina had been
scuttled is the wish of Chilon for Cythera.
Herod. 7, 235.]

[Note: This impression, erroneous as it seems,
was contravened in a letter from Mr. WM. A.
COURTENAY, Mayor and historian of Charleston,
who wrote to me: "The W. L. I. was named for
George Washington. The 22d of February was
celebrated as the anniversary from 1807-92
(thirty years ago in Fort Sumter under fire),
and the connection of the corps with Col. Wm.
Washington was not until April, 1827, on the
presentation of the Eutaw flag to the corps by
his widow." However, the memory of the lesser
Washington is still kept alive, and the William
Washington house is still one of the show
places of my native city. As a further
illustration of local patriotism I may add that
the Charleston boys were more excited over the
28th of June, the battle of Fort Moultrie, than
over the national Fourth of July.]

In claiming this individuality, nothing more is
claimed for Virginia and for South Carolina
than would be conceded to Massachusetts and
Connecticut; and we believed then that
Massachusetts and Connecticut would not have
behaved otherwise than we did, if the parts had
been reversed. The brandished sword would have
shown what manner of _placida quies_
Massachusetts would have ensued, if demands had

been made on her at all commensurate with the Federal demands on Virginia. These older Southern States were proud of their history, and they showed their pride by girding at their neighbors. South Carolina had her fling at Georgia, her fling at North Carolina; and the wish that the little State had been scuttled at an early day was a plagiarism from classical literature that might have emanated from the South as well as from the North. Virginia assumed a superiority that was resented by her Southern sisters as well as by her Northern partners. The Old North State derided the pretensions of the commonwealths that flanked her on either side, and Georgia was not slow to give South Carolina as good as she sent. All this seemed to be harmless banter, but the rivalry was old enough and strong enough to encourage the hopes of the Union leaders that the Confederacy would split along state lines. The cohesive power of the Revolutionary war was not sufficiently strong to make the States sink their contributions to the common cause in the common glory. Washington was the one national hero, and yet the Washington Light Infantry of Charleston was named, not after the illustrious George, but after his kinsman, William. The story of Lexington and Concord and Bunker Hill did not thrill the South Carolinian of an earlier day, and those great achievements were actually criticized. Who were Putnam and Stark that South Carolinians should worship them, when they had a Marion and a Sumter of their own? Vermont went wild, the other day, over Bennington as she did not over the centenary of the surrender at Yorktown. Take away this local patriotism and you take out all the color that is left in American life. That the local patriotism may not only consist with a wider patriotism, but may serve as a most important element in wider patriotism, is true. Witness the strong local life in the old provinces of France. No student of history, no painter of manners, can neglect it. In Gerfaut, a novel written before the Franco-Prussian war, Charles de Bernard represents an Alsatian shepherd as saying, "I am not French; I am Alsatian,"--

"_trait de patriotisme de clocher assez commun dans la belle province du Rhin_," adds the author, little dreaming of the national significance of that "patriotisme de clocher." The Breton's love of his home is familiar to every one who has read his Renan, and Blanche Willis Howard, in Guenn, makes her priest exclaim, "Monsieur, I would fight with France against any other nation, but I would fight with Brittany against France. I love France. I am a Frenchman. But first of all I am a Breton." The Provençal speaks of France as if she were a foreign country, and fights for her as if she were his alone. What is true of France is true in a measure of England. Devonshire men are notoriously Devonshire men first and last. If this is true of what have become integral parts of kingdom or republic by centuries of incorporation, what is to be said of the States that had never renounced their sovereignty, that had only suspended it in part?

The example of state pride set by the older States was not lost on the younger Southern States, and the Alabamian and the Mississippian lived in the same faith as did the stock from which they sprang; and the community of views, of interest, of social order, soon made a larger unit and prepared the way for a true nationality, and with the nationality a great conflict. The heterogeneousness of the elements that made up the Confederacy did not prove the great source of weakness that was expected. The Border States looked on the world with different eyes from the Gulf States. The Virginia farmer and the Creole planter of Louisiana were of different strains; and yet there was a solidarity that has never failed to surprise the few Northerners who penetrated the South for study and pleasure. There was an extraordinary ramification of family and social ties throughout the Southern States, and a few minutes' conversation sufficed to place any member of the social organism from Virginia to Texas. Great schools, like the University of Virginia, within the Southern border did much to foster the community of feeling, and while there were not a few Southerners at Harvard and Yale, and while Princeton was almost a Southern college, an education in the North did not seem to nationalize the Southerner. On the contrary, as in the universities of the Middle Ages, groups were formed in accordance with nativity; and sectional lines, though effaced at certain points, were strengthened at others. There may have been a certain broadening of view; there was no weakening of the home ties. West Point made fewer converts to this side and to that than did the Northern wives of Southern husbands, the Southern wives of Northern husbands.

All this is doubtless controvertible, and what has been written may serve only to amuse or to disgust those who are better versed in the facts of our history and keener analysts of its laws. All that I vouch for is the feeling; the only point that I have tried to make is the simple fact that, right or wrong, we were fully persuaded in our own minds, and that there was no lurking suspicion of any moral weakness in our cause. Nothing could be holier than the cause, nothing more imperative than the duty of upholding it. There were those in the South who, when they saw the issue of the war, gave up their faith in God, but not their faith in the cause.

It is perfectly possible to be fully persuaded in one's own mind without the passionate desire to make converts that animates the born preacher, and any one may be excused from preaching when he recognizes the existence of a mental or moral color-blindness with which it is not worth while to argue. There is no umpire to decide which of the disputants is color-blind, and the discussion is apt to degenerate into a wearisome reiteration of points which neither party will concede. Now this matter of allegiance is just such a question. Open the October number of The Atlantic and read the sketch of General Thomas, whom many military men on the Southern side consider to have been the ablest of all the Federal generals. He was, as every one knows, a Virginian, and it seemed to us that his being a Virginian was remembered against him in the Federal councils. "His severance," says the writer in The Atlantic, "from family and State was a keen trial, but 'his duty was clear from the beginning.' To his vision there was but one country,--the United States of America. He had few or no friends at the North. Its political policy had not seemed to him to be wise. But he could serve under no flag except that which he had pledged his honor to uphold." Passing over the quiet assumption that the North was the United States of America, which sufficiently characterizes the view of the writer, let us turn to the contrast which would at once have suggested itself even if it had not been brought forward by the eulogist of Thomas. A greater than Thomas decided the question at the same time, and decided it the other way. To Lee's vision there was but one course open to a Virginian, and the pledge that he had given when Virginia was one of the United States of America had ceased to bind him when Virginia withdrew from the compact. His duty was clear from the hour when to remain in the army would have been to draw his sword against a people to whom he was "indissolubly bound."

[Note: "I think it is not unsafe to assert that nowhere did the original spirit of State Sovereignty and allegiance to the State then survive in greater intensity and more unquestioning form than in Virginia--the 'Old Dominion'--the mother of States and of Presidents.

"State pride, a sense of individuality, has immemorially entered more largely and more intensely into Virginia and Virginians than into any other section or community of the United States. Only in South Carolina and among Carolinians, on the trans-Atlantic continent, was a somewhat similar sense of locality and obligation of descent to be found. There was in it a flavour of the Hidalgo, or of the pride which the MacGregors and Campbells took in their clan and country. In other words, the Virginian and Carolinian had in the middle of the last century, not to any appreciable extent, undergone nationalization."--CHAS. FRANCIS ADAMS, Trans-Atlantic Historical Solidarity p. 137.

I have referred to Mr. ADAMS repeatedly because as a man of my time and nearly of my age he understood the difficulty of moving the point of view fifty years backward.]

These contrasted cases are indeed convenient tests for color-blindness. There may "arise a generation in Virginia," or even a generation of Virginians, "who will learn and confess" that "Thomas loved Virginia as well as the sons she has preferred to honor, and served her better." But no representative Virginian shares that prophetic vision; the color-blindness, on whichever side it is, has not yielded to treatment during the twenty-five years that have elapsed since the close of the war, and may as well be accepted for an indefinite period. When social relations were resumed between the North and the South,--they followed slowly the resumption of business relations,-- what we should call the color-blindness of the other side often manifested itself in a delicate reticence on the part of our Northern friends; and as the war had by no means constituted their lives as it had constituted ours for four long years, the success in avoiding the disagreeable topic would have been considerable, if it had not been for awkward allusions on the part of the Southerners, who, having been shut out for all that time from the study of literature and art and other elegant and uncompromising subjects, could hardly keep from speaking of this and that incident of the war. Whereupon a discreet, or rather an embarrassed silence, as if a pardoned convict had playfully referred to the arson or burglary, not to say worse, that had been the cause of his seclusion.

[Note: In these days of mutual understanding and mutual forgiveness, I shall hardly be believed when I say that as late as 1885, twenty years after the close of the war, some of my Northern friends who had been taught the duty of "making treason odious" advised me to suppress or modify the following passage in my Introduction to Pindar (p. xii) as savoring of disloyalty:

The man whose love for his country knows no local root, is a man whose love for his country is a poor abstraction; and it is no discredit to Pindar that he went honestly with his state in the struggle. It was no treason to Medize before there was a Greece, and the Greece that came out of the Persian war was a very different thing from the cantons that ranged themselves on this side and on that of a quarrel which, we may be sure, bore another aspect to those who stood aloof from it than it wears in the eyes of moderns, who have all learned to be Hellenic patriots. A little experience of a losing side might aid historical vision. That Pindar should have had an intense admiration of the New Greece, should have felt the impulse of the grand period that followed Salamis and Plataia, should have appreciated the woe that would have come on Greece had the Persians been successful, and should have seen the finger of God in the new evolution of Hellas--all this is not incompatible with an attitude during the Persian war that those who see the end and do not understand the beginning may not consider respectable.]

Some fifteen years ago Mr. Lowell was lecturing in Baltimore, and during the month of his stay I learned to know the charm of his manner and the delight of his conversation. If I had been even more prejudiced than I was, I could not have withstood that easy grace, that winning cordiality. Every one knew where he had stood

during the war, and how he had wielded the
flail of his "lashing hail" against the South
and the Southern cause and "Southern
sympathizers." But that warfare was over for
him, and out of kindly regard for my feelings
he made no allusion to the great quarrel, with
two exceptions. Once, just before he left
Baltimore, he was talking as no other man could
talk about the Yankee dialect, and turning to
me he said with a half smile and a deep twinkle
in his eye, "I should like to have you read
what I have written about the Yankee dialect,
but I am afraid you might not like the
context." A few days afterwards I received from
him the well-known preface to the Second Series
of The Biglow Papers, cut out from the volume.
It was a graceful concession to Southern
weakness, and after all I may have been
mistaken in thinking that I could read the
Second Series as literature, just as I should
read the Anti-Jacobin or the Two-penny Post
Bag. In fact, on looking into the Second Series
again, I must confess that I cannot even now
discover the same merits that I could not help
acknowledging in the First Series, which I read
for the first time in 1850, when I was a
student in Berlin. By that time I had recovered
from my boyish enthusiasm over the Mexican war,
and as my party had been successful, I could
afford to enjoy the wit and humor of the book,
from the inimitable Notices of an Independent
Press to the last utterance of Birdofredum
Sawin; and I have always remembered enough of
the contents to make a psychological study of
the Second Series a matter of interest, if it
were not for other things.

On the second occasion we were passing together
under the shadow of the Washington Monument,
and the name of Lee came by some chance into
the current of talk. Here Mr. Lowell could not
refrain from expressing his view of Lee's
course in turning against the government to
which he had sworn allegiance. Doubtless he
felt it to be his duty to emphasize his
conviction as to a vital clause of his creed,
but it instantly became evident that this was a

theme that could not be profitably pursued, and we walked in silence the rest of the way,--the author of the line

Virginia gave us this imperial man,

and the follower of that other imperial man Virginia gave the world; both honest, each believing the other hopelessly wrong, but absolutely sincere.

[Note: Of many consentient utterances I select this one by a prominent Southerner:

"The Confederate soldiers did not go to war to perpetuate slavery. Most of them never owned a slave, and our hero, Gen. ROBERT E. LEE, said that if he owned every one of the slaves in the South he would give them for the preservation of the Union. It was not for the slaves they fought, but for principle, for their homes and native land."--T. F. GOODE, Confederate Banquet, January 19, 1893.]

Scant allusion has been made in this paper to the subject of slavery, which bulks so large in almost every study of the war. A similar scantiness of allusion to slavery is noticeable in the Memorial volume, to which I have already referred; a volume which was prepared, not to produce an impression on the Northern mind, but to indulge a natural desire to honor the fallen soldiers of the Confederacy; a book written by friends for friends. The rights of the State and the defence of the country are mentioned at every turn; "the peculiar institution" is merely touched on here and there, except in one passage in which a Virginian speaker maintains that as a matter of dollars and cents it would be better for Virginia to give up her slaves than to set up a separate government, with all the cost of a standing army which the conservation of slavery would make necessary. This silence, which might be misunderstood, is plain enough to a Southern man. Slavery was

simply a test case, and except as a test case
it is too complicated a question to be dealt
with at the close of a paper which is already
too long. Except as a test case it is
impossible to speak of the Southern view of the
institution, for we were not all of the same
mind.

[Note: "When, within our memory, some flippant
Senator [Hammond] wished to taunt the people of
this country by calling them 'the mudsills of
society,' he paid them ignorantly a true
praise; for good men are as the green plain of
the earth is, as the rocks and the beds of the
rivers are, the foundation and flooring and
sills of the State."--R. W. EMERSON, Atlantic
Monthly, January, 1892, p. 33.

In an oration delivered before the United
Confederate Veterans, June 14, 1904, RANDOLPH
HARRISON McKIM, a former pupil of mine and a
cousin of my college mates mentioned on page
16, says: "The political head of the
Confederacy entered upon the war, foreseeing
(February, 1861) the eventual loss of his
slaves, and the military head of the
Confederacy actually set his slaves free before
the war was half over."--The Motives and Aims
of the Soldiers of the South in the Civil War,
p. 28. The whole oration confirms the positions
taken in this article.]

There were theorists who maintained that a
society based on the rock of slavery was the
best possible in a world where there must be a
lowest order; and the doctrine of the "mud-
sill" as propounded by a leading thinker of
this school evoked mud volcanoes all over the
North. Scriptural arguments in defence of
slavery formed a large part of the literature
of the subject, and the hands of Southern
clergymen were upheld by their conservative
brothers beyond the border.

Some who had read the signs of the times
otherwise knew that slavery was doomed by the
voice of the world, and that no theory of

society could withstand the advance of the new spirit; and if the secrets of all hearts could have been revealed, our enemies would have been astounded to see how many thousands and tens of thousands in the Southern States felt the crushing burden and the awful responsibility of the institution which we were supposed to be defending with the melodramatic fury of pirate kings. We were born to this social order, we had to do our duty in it according to our lights, and this duty was made indefinitely more difficult by the interference of those who, as we thought, could not understand the conditions of the problem, and who did not have to bear the expense of the experiments they proposed.

There were the practical men who saw in the negro slave an efficient laborer in a certain line of work, and there were the practical men who doubted the economic value of our system as compared with that of the free States, and whom the other practical men laughed to scorn.

There was the small and eminently respectable body of benevolent men who promoted the scheme of African colonization, of which great things were expected in my boyhood. The manifest destiny of slavery in America was the regeneration of Africa.

The people at large had no theory, and the practice varied as much in the relation of master and servant as it varied in other family relations. Too much tragedy and too much idyl have been imported into the home life of the Southern people; but this is not the place to reduce poetry to prose.

On one point, however, all parties in the South were agreed, and the vast majority of the people of the North--before the war. The abolitionist proper was considered not so much the friend of the negro as the enemy of society. As the war went on, and the abolitionist saw the "glory of the Lord" revealed in a way he had never hoped for, he

saw at the same time, or rather ought to have
seen, that the order he had lived to destroy
could not have been a system of hellish wrong
and fiendish cruelty; else the prophetic vision
of the liberators would have been fulfilled,
and the horrors of San Domingo would have
polluted this fair land. For the negro race
does not deserve undivided praise for its
conduct during the war. Let some small part of
the credit be given to the masters, not all to
the finer qualities of their "brothers in
black." The school in which the training was
given is closed, and who wishes to open it? Its
methods were old-fashioned and were sadly
behind the times, but the old schoolmasters
turned out scholars who, in certain branches of
moral philosophy, were not inferior to the
graduates of the new university.

[Note: A recent historian of the war, PAXSON
(The Civil War, p. 248), says: "Northern
revenge in the guise of the preservation of the
dearly won Union was worse for the South than
the war."

CHARLES FRANCIS ADAMS, _l. c._, p. 165:
"Outrages, and humiliations worse than outrage,
of the period of so-called reconstruction but
actual servile domination."

_L. c._, p. 173: "It may not unfairly be
doubted whether a people prostrate after civil
conflict has ever received severer measure than
was dealt out to the so-called reconstructed
Confederate States during the years immediately
succeeding the close of strife. That the policy
inspired at the time a feeling of bitter
resentment in the South was no cause for
wonder." To me the cause for wonder was and is
that a Virginian of Virginians should have
wholly forgotten the bitterness, as is evinced
by the following passage in an oration
delivered shortly after the publication of this
article:

"No such peace as our peace ever followed
immediately upon such a war as our war. The

exhausted South was completely at the mercy of the vigorous North, and yet the sound of the last gun had scarcely died away when not only peace, but peace and goodwill were re-established, and the victors and the vanquished took up the work of repairing the damages of war and advancing the common welfare of the whole country, as if the old relations, social, commercial and political between the people of the two sections had never been disturbed."-- CHARLES MARSHALL, of Lee's Staff, on Grant, May 30, 1892.]

[Note: It was out of the bitterness of this reconstruction period that I penned the following sonnet to the memory of JOHN M. DANIEL, editor of the Richmond Examiner, to which paper I contributed more than threescore editorial articles during the year 1863-4:

                    DIS   MANIBUS
I. M. D.

We miss your pen of fire, whose cloven tongue
Illum'd the good and blasted what was base.
We miss you, fearless fighter for our race,
Your arrows words, your bow a will highstrung.
We miss you, for you tower'd from among
The herd of writers with that careless grace
That springs from undisputed strength. Your place
Is vacant still. Your bow is still uphung.
'Tis well. This were no time for you. The strings
Of your proud heart forefelt the blow and broke;
And when you died, 'twas better thus to die
Than live to see this swarm of crawling things,
And burn with words that must remain unspoke
Where "art is tongue-tied by authority."]

[Note: The school was the Episcopal High School near Alexandria, Virginia; the principal, the late L. M. BLACKFORD.]

[Note: Ov. Her. 3, 106:

According to Ovid, Briseis was a non-Greek. _Littera_, she writes (v. 2), _vix bene barbarica Graeca notata manu_. According to recent authorities, she was a Lesbian girl. We know from Homer that Achilles was musical as Odysseus was not.

[Greek: ton d' heuron phrena terpomenon phormingi ligeiê, kali, daidaleê, epi d' argyreon zygon êen.]--Il. 9, 185-6.]

[Note: Lesbos was an island consecrated to music from the days of Orpheus, and we can imagine the lovers singing together and Achilles solacing his loneliness by chanting to Patroclus the praises of his lost love.]

[Note: The valued friend was and is ARCHER ANDERSON, of Richmond, Virginia.]

[Note: "Why is it that wherever one goes in all parts of England one always finds--thoroughly as I believe the institution of slavery is detested in this country--every man sympathizing strongly with the Southerners, and wishing them all success? We do so for this reason ... Englishmen love liberty, and the Southerner is fighting, not only for his life, but for that which is dearer than life, for liberty; he is fighting against one of the most grinding, one of the most galling, one of the most irritating attempts to establish tyrannical government that ever disgraced the history of the World."--G. W. BENTINCK, quoted by CHAS. FRANCIS ADAMS, _l. c._, p. 111.]

I have tried in this paper to reproduce the past and its perspective, to show how the men of my time and of my environment looked at the problems that confronted us. It has been a painful and, I fear, a futile task. So far as I have reproduced the perspective for myself it has been a revival of sorrows such as this generation cannot understand; it has recalled the hours when it gave one a passion for death, a shame of life, to read our bulletins. And how could I hope to reproduce that perspective for others, for men who belong to another generation and another region, when so many men who lived the same life and fought on the same side have themselves lost the point of view not only of the beginning of the war, but also of the end of the war, not only of the inexpressible exaltation, but of the unutterable degradation? They have forgotten what a strange world the survivors of the conflict had to face. If the State had been ours still, the foundations of the earth would not have been out of course; but the State was a military district, and the Confederacy had ceased to exist. The generous policy which would have restored the State and made a new union possible, which would have disentwined much of the passionate clinging to the past, was crossed by the death of the only man who could have carried it through, if even he could have carried it through; and years of trouble had to pass before the current of national life ran freely through the Southern States. It was before this circuit was complete that the principal of one of the chief schools of Virginia set up a tablet to the memory of the "old boys" who had perished in the war,--it was a list the length of which few Northern colleges could equal,--and I was asked to furnish a motto. Those who know classic literature at all know that for patriotism and friendship mottoes are not far to seek, but during the war I felt as I had never felt before the meaning of many a classic sentence. The motto came from Ovid, whom many call a frivolous poet; but the frivolous Roman was after all a Roman, and he was young when he wrote the line,--too young not to feel the generous swell of true feeling. It was written of the dead brothers of Briseis:--

Qui bene pro patria cum patriaque iacent.

The sentiment found an echo at the time, deserved an echo at the time. Now it is a

sentiment without an echo, and last year a
valued personal friend of mine, in an eloquent
oration, a noble tribute to the memory of our
great captain, a discourse full of the glory of
the past, the wisdom of the present, the hope
of the future, rebuked the sentiment as idle in
its despair. As well rebuke a cry of anguish, a
cry of desolation out of the past. For those
whose names are recorded on that tablet the
line is but too true. For those of us who
survive it has ceased to have the import that
it once had, for we have learned to work
resolutely for the furtherance of all that is
good in the wider life that has been opened to
us by the issue of the war, without
complaining, without repining.

That the cause we fought for and our brothers
died for was the cause of civil liberty, and
not the cause of human slavery, is a thesis
which we feel ourselves bound to maintain
whenever our motives are challenged or
misunderstood, if only for our children's sake.
But even that will not long be necessary, for
the vindication of our principles will be made
manifest in the working out of the problems
with which the republic has to grapple. If,
however, the effacement of state lines and the
complete centralization of the government shall
prove to be the wisdom of the future, the
poetry of life will still find its home in the
old order, and those who loved their State best
will live longest in song and legend,--song yet
unsung, legend not yet crystallized.

A SOUTHERNER IN THE PELOPONNESIAN WAR

I

[Note: The ambitious title, "Two Wars," has
been restored to the headline by typographical
pressure.]

[Note: History is philosophy teaching by examples. Ps. Dionys. xi, 2 (399R): [Greek: historia philosophia estin ek paradeigmatôn].]

I had intended to call this study Two Wars, but I was afraid lest I should be under the domination of the title, and an elaborate comparison of the Peloponnesian War and the War between the States would undoubtedly have led to no little sophistication of the facts. Historical parallel bars are usually set up for exhibiting feats of mental agility. The mental agility is often moral suppleness, and nobody expects a critical examination of the parallelism itself. He was not an historian of the first rank, but a phrase-making rhetorician, who is responsible for the current saying, History is philosophy teaching by examples. This definition is about as valuable as some of those other definitions that express one art in terms of another: poetry in terms of painting, and painting in terms of poetry. "Architecture is frozen music" does not enable us to understand either perpendicular Gothic or a fugue of Bach; and when an historian defines history in terms of philosophy, or a philosopher philosophy in terms of history, you may be on the lookout for sophistication. Your philosophical historian points his moral by adorning his tale. Your historical philosopher allows no zigzags in the march of his evolution.

In like manner, the attempt to express one war in terms of another is apt to lead to a wresting of facts. No two wars are as like as two peas. Yet as any two marriages in society will yield a certain number of resemblances, so will any two wars in history, whether war itself be regarded as abstract or concrete,--a question that seems to have exercised some grammatical minds, and ought therefore to be settled before any further step is taken in this disquisition, which is the disquisition of a grammarian. Now most persons would pronounce war an abstract, but one excellent manual with which I am acquainted sets it down as a

Civil War Classic Library

concrete, and I have often thought that the author must have known something practically about war. At all events, to those who have seen the midday sun darkened by burning homesteads, and wheatfields illuminated by stark forms in blue and gray, war is sufficiently concrete. The very first dead soldier one sees, enemy or friend, takes war forever out of the category of abstracts.

[Note: JOHN AUGUSTINE WASHINGTON, 'as always in the Washington family' W. GORDON McCABE.]

When I was a student abroad, American novices used to be asked in jest, "Is this your first ruin?" "Is this your first nightingale?" I am not certain that I can place my first ruin or my first nightingale, but I can recall my first dead man on the battlefield. We were making an advance on the enemy's position near Huttonsville. Nothing, by the way, could have been more beautiful than the plan, which I was privileged to see; and as we neared the objective point, it was a pleasure to watch how column after column, marching by this road and that, converged to the rendezvous. It was as if some huge spider were gathering its legs about the victim. The special order issued breathed a spirit of calm resolution worthy of the general commanding and his troops. Nobody that I remember criticised the tautological expression, "The progress of this army must be forward." We were prepared for a hard fight, for we knew that the enemy was strongly posted. Most of us were to be under fire for the first time, and there was some talk about the chances of the morrow as we lay down to sleep. Moralizing of that sort gets less and less common with experience in the business, and this time the moralizing may have seemed to some premature. But wherever the minié ball sang its diabolical mosquito song there was death in the air, and I was soon to see brought into camp, under a flag of truce, the lifeless body of the heir of Mount Vernon, whose graceful riding I had envied a few days before. However, there was no serious fighting. The advance on the enemy's position had developed more strength in front than we had counted on, or some of the spider's legs had failed to close in. A misleading report had been brought to headquarters. A weak point in the enemy's line had been reinforced. Who knows? The best laid plans are often thwarted by the merest trifles,--an insignificant puddle, a jingling canteen. This game of war is a hit or miss game, after all. A certain fatalism is bred thereby, and it is well to set out with a stock of that article. So our resolute advance became a forced reconnaissance, greatly to the chagrin of the younger and more ardent spirits. We found out exactly where the enemy was, and declined to have anything further to do with him for the time being. But in finding him we had to clear the ground and drive in the pickets. One picket had been posted at the end of a loop in a chain of valleys. The road we followed skirted the base of one range of hills. The house which served as the headquarters of the picket was on the other side. A meadow as level as a board stretched between. I remember seeing a boy come out and catch a horse, while we were advancing. Somehow it seemed to be a trivial thing to do just then. I knew better afterwards. Our skirmishers had done their work, had swept the woods on either side clean, and the pickets had fallen back on the main body; but not all of them. One man, if not more, had only had time to fall dead. The one I saw, the first, was a young man, not thirty, I should judge, lying on his back, his head too low for comfort. He had been killed outright, and there was no distortion of feature. No more peaceful faces than one sees at times on the battlefield, and sudden death, despite the Litany, is not the least enviable exit. In this case there was something like a mild surprise on the countenance. The rather stolid face could never have been very expressive. An unposted letter was found on the dead man's body. It was written in German, and I was asked to interpret it, in case it should contain any important information. There was no important information; just messages to friends and kindred, just the trivialities of camp life.

The man was an invader, and in my eyes deserved an invader's doom. If sides had been changed, he would have been a rebel, and would have deserved a rebel's doom. I was not stirred to the depths by the sight, but it gave me a lesson in grammar, and war has ever been concrete to me from that time on. The horror I did not feel at first grew steadily. "A sweet thing," says Pindar, "is war to those that have not tried it."

II

[Note: SPANGENBERG was a literary "bummer." The real author was one ANDREAS GUARNA of Salerno. See FRÄNKEL, Zeitschrift für Litteraturgeschichte, xiii, 242.]

[Note: Pindar's words are: [Greek: glyky d' apeiroisi polemos].]

Concrete or abstract, there are general resemblances between any two wars, and so war lends itself readily to allegories. Every one has read Bunyan's Holy War. Not every one has read Spangenberg's Grammatical War. It is an ingenious performance, which fell into my hands many years after I had gone forth to see and to feel what war was like. In Spangenberg's Grammatical War the nouns and the verbs are the contending parties. Poeta is king of the nouns, and Amo king of the verbs. There is a regular debate between the two sovereigns. The king of the verbs summons the adverbs to his help, the king of the nouns the pronouns. The camps are pitched, the forces marshalled. The neutral power, participle, is invoked by both parties, but declines to send open assistance to either, hoping that in this contest between noun and verb the third party will acquire the rule over the whole territory of language. After a final summons on the part of the king of the verbs, and a fierce response from the rival monarch, active hostilities begin. We read of raids and forays. Prisoners are treated with contumely, and their skirts are docked as in the Biblical narrative. Treachery adds excitement to the situation. Skirmishes precede the great engagement, in which the nouns are worsted, though they have come off with some of the spoils of war; and peace is made on terms dictated by Priscian, Servius, and Donatus. Spangenberg's Grammatical War is a not uninteresting, not uninstructive squib, and the salt of it, or saltpetre of it, has not all evaporated after the lapse of some three centuries. There are bits that remind one of the Greco-Turkish war of a few weeks ago.

[Note: Terror and Affright, Il. 15, 19: [Greek: hôs phato kai rh' hippous keleto Deimon te Phobon te | zeugnymen]. These horses of Ares furnished the names Deimos and Phobos for the two satellites of the planet Mars. Such traces of familiarity with the classics are refreshing to one who lives in an age when allusion is under the ban. How many appreciate the appropriateness of the Baltimore County Timonium, named after Mark Antony's growlery in Plutarch? Not many of the sports who some years ago laid their bets on Irex recalled the line of the Odyssey 13, 86:

[Greek:

                    oude   ken   irêx
kirkos homartêseien elaphrotatos peteênôn.]]

But there is no military science in Bunyan's Holy War nor in Spangenberg's Grammatical War: why should there be? Practical warfare is rough work. To frighten, to wound, to kill,--these three abide under all forms of military doctrine, and the greatest of these is frightening. Ares, the god of war, has two satellites, Terror and Affright. Fear is the Gorgon's head. The serpents are very real, very effective, in their way, but logically they are unessential tresses. The Gorgon stares you out

of countenance, and that suffices. The object
is the removal of an obstacle. Killing and
wounding are but means to an end. Hand-to-hand
fighting is rare, and it would be easy to count
the instances in which cavalry meets the shock
of cavalry. Crossing sabres is not a common
pastime in the red game of war. It makes a fine
picture, to be sure, the finer for the rarity
of the thing itself.

To frighten, to wound, to kill, being the
essential processes, war amounts to the same
thing the world over, world of time and world
of space. Whether death or disability comes by
Belgian ball or Spencer bullet, by the stone of
a Balearic slinger, by a bolt from a crossbow,
is a matter of detail which need not trouble
the philosophic mind, and the ancients showed
their sense in ascribing fear to divine
inspiration.

[Note: The Scandinavian scholar, JESPERSEN.]

If the processes of war are primitive, the
causes of war are no less so. It has been
strikingly said of late by a Scandinavian
scholar that "language was born in the
courting-days of mankind: the first utterance
of speech <was> something between the nightly
love-lyrics of puss upon the tiles and the
melodious love-songs of the nightingale." "War,
the father of all things," goes back to the
same origin as language. The serenade is
matched by the battle-cry. The fight between
two cock-pheasants for the love of a hen-
pheasant is war in its last analysis, in its
primal manifestation. Selfish hatred is at the
bottom of it. It is the hell-fire to which we
owe the heat that is necessary to some of the
noblest as to some of the vilest manifestations
of human nature. Righteous indignation, sense
of injustice, sympathy with the oppressed,
consecration to country, fine words all, fine
things, but so many of the men who represent
these fine things perish. It wrings the heart
at a distance of more than thirty years to
think of those who have fallen, and love still

maintains passionately that they were the best. At any rate, they were among the best, and both sides are feeling the loss to this day, not only in the men themselves, but in the sons that should have been born to them.

Any two wars, then, will yield a sufficient number of resemblances, in killed, wounded, and missing, in the elemental matter of hatred, or, if you choose to give it a milder name, rivalry. These things are of the essence of war, and the manifestations run parallel even in the finer lines. One cock-pheasant finds the drumming of another cock-pheasant a very irritating sound, Chanticleer objects to the note of Chanticleer, and the more articulate human being is rasped by the voice of his neighbor. The Attic did not like the broad Boeotian speech. Parson Evans's "seese and putter" were the bitterest ingredients in Falstaff's dose of humiliation. "Yankee twang" and "Southern drawl" incited as well as echoed hostility.

[Note: Ach. 527.]

Borderers are seldom friends. "An Attic neighbor" is a Greek proverb. Kentucky and Ohio frown at each other across the river. Cincinnati looks down on Covington, and Covington glares at Cincinnati. Aristophanes, in his mocking way, attributes the Peloponnesian war to a kidnapping affair between Athens and Megara. The underground railroad preceded the aboveground railroad in the history of the great American conflict.

There were jealousies enough between Athens and Sparta in the olden times, which correspond to our colonial days, and in the Persian war, which was in a sense the Greek war of independence. In like manner the chronicles of our Revolutionary period show that there was abundance of bad blood between Northern colonies and Southern colonies. The Virginian planter whom all have agreed to make the one national hero was after all a Virginian, and

Virginians have not forgotten the impatient
utterances of the "imperial man" on the soil of
Massachusetts and in the streets of New York.
Nobody takes Knickerbocker's History of New
York seriously, as owlish historians are wont
to take Aristophanes. Why not? We accept the
hostility of Attica and Boeotia, of Attica and
Megara; and there are no more graphic chapters
than those which set forth the enmity between
New York and Maryland, between New Amsterdam
and Connecticut.

[Note: The Peloponnesians called it the Attic
War (Thuc. 5, 28, 3); the Ionians the Doric
War. In a recent number of the Jahrbücher,
xxxv, No. 2 (1915), there is a discussion of
the name of the Peloponnesian War apropos of
the present "World-war," or, if you choose,
"Wirrwarr." For our war the misnomer "The Civil
War" has been adopted as the official
designation.]

Business is often more potent than blood.
Nullification, the forerunner of disunion, rose
from a question of tariff. The echoes had not
died out when I woke to conscious life. I knew
that I was the son of a nullifier, and the
nephew of a Union man. It was whispered that
our beloved family physician found it prudent
to withdraw from the public gaze for a while,
and that my uncle's windows were broken by the
palmettoes of a nullification procession; and I
can remember from my boyhood days how
unreconciled citizens of Charleston shook their
fists at the revenue cutter and its "foreign
flag." Such an early experience enables one to
understand our war better. It enables one to
understand the Peloponnesian war better, the
struggle between the union of which Athens was
the mistress and the confederacy of which
Sparta was the head. Non-intercourse between
Athens and Megara was the first stage. The
famous Megarian decree of Pericles, which
closed the market of Athens to Megarians, gave
rise to angry controversy, and the refusal to
rescind that decree led to open war. But Megara
was little more than a pretext. The subtle

influence of Corinth was potent. The great merchant city of Greece dreaded the rise of Athens to dominant commercial importance, and in the conflict between the Corinthian brass and the Attic clay, the clay was shattered. Corinth does not show her hand much in the Peloponnesian war. She figures at the beginning, and then disappears. But the old mole is at work the whole time, and what the Peloponnesians called the Attic war, and the Attics the Peloponnesian war, might have been called the Corinthian war. The exchange, the banking-house, were important factors then as now. "Sinews of war" is a classical expression. The popular cry of "Persian gold" was heard in the Peloponnesian war as the popular cry of "British gold" is heard now.

True, there was no slavery question in the Peloponnesian war, for antique civilization without slavery is hardly thinkable; but after all, the slavery question belongs ultimately to the sphere of economics. The humanitarian spirit, set free by the French Revolution, was at work in the Southern States as in the Northern States, but it was hampered by economic considerations. Virginia, as every one knows, was on the verge of becoming a free State. Colonization flourished in my boyhood. A friend of my father's left him trustee for his "servants," as we called them. They were quartered opposite our house in Charleston, and the pickaninnies were objects of profound interest to the children of the neighborhood. One or two letters came from the emigrants after they reached Liberia. Then silence fell on the African farm.

Some of the most effective anti-slavery reformers were Charlestonians by birth and breeding. I cannot say that Grimké was a popular name, but homage was paid to the talent of Frederick, as I remember only too well, for I had to learn a speech of his by heart, as a schoolboy exercise. But the economic conditions of the South were not favorable to the spread of the ideas represented by the Grimkés. The slavery question kept alive the spirit that manifested itself in the tariff question. State rights were not suffered to slumber. The Southerner resented Northern dictation as Pericles resented Lacedæmonian dictation, and our Peloponnesian war began.

III

The processes of the two wars, then, were the same,--killing, wounding, frightening. The causes of the two wars resolved themselves into the elements of hatred. The details of the two wars meet at many points; only one must be on one's guard against merely fanciful, merely external resemblances.

In 1860 I spent a few days in Holland, and among my various excursions in that fascinating country I took a solitary trip on a _treckschuit_ from Amsterdam to Delft. Holland was so true to Dutch pictures that there was a retrospective delight in the houses and in the people. There was a charm in the very signs, in the names of the villas; for my knowledge of Dutch had not passed beyond the stage at which the Netherlandish tongue seems to be an English-German Dictionary, disguised in strong waters. But the thing that struck me most was the general aspect of the country. Everywhere gates. Nowhere fences. The gates guarded the bridges and the canals were the fences, but the canals and the low bridges were not to be seen at a distance, and the visual effect was that of isolated gates. It was an absurd landscape even after the brain had made the necessary corrections.

In the third year of the war I was not far from Fredericksburg. The country had been stripped, and the forlorn region was a sad contrast to the smug prosperity of Holland. And yet of a sudden the Dutch landscape flashed upon my inward eye, for Spottsylvania, like Holland, was dotted with fenceless gates. The rails of the inclosures had long before gone to feed bivouac fires, but the great gates were too solidly constructed to tempt marauders. It was an absurd landscape, an absurd parallel.

Historical parallels are often no better. When one compares two languages of the same family, the first impression is that of similarity. It is hard for the novice to keep his Italian and his Spanish apart. The later and more abiding impression is that of dissimilarity. A total stranger confounds twins in whom the members of the household find but vague likeness. There is no real resemblance between the two wars we are contemplating outside the inevitable features of all armed conflicts, and we must be on our guard against the sophistication deprecated in the beginning of this study. And yet one coming fresh to a comparison of the Peloponnesian war and the war between the States might see a striking similarity, such as I saw between the Dutch landscape and the landscape in Spottsylvania.

The Peloponnesian war, like our war, was a war between two leagues, a Northern Union and a Southern Confederacy. The Northern Union, represented by Athens, was a naval power. The Southern Confederacy, under the leadership of Sparta, was a land power. The Athenians represented the progressive element, the Spartans the conservative. The Athenians believed in a strong centralized government. The Lacedæmonians professed greater regard for autonomy. A little ingenuity, a good deal of hardihood, might multiply such futilities indefinitely. In fact, it would be possible to write the story of our Peloponnesian war in phrases of Thucydides, and I should not be surprised if such a task were a regular school exercise at Eton or at Rugby. Why, it was but the other day that Professor Tyrrell, of Dublin, translated a passage from Lowell's Biglow Papers into choice Aristophanese.

[Note: According to _fama clamosa_, Winfield was originally Wingfield, a very common Virginian name. The classical parallel of

Tromes and Atrometos will suggest itself to every one who has read Demosthenes. Dem. 18, 129.]

Unfortunately, such feats, as I have already said, imperil one's intellectual honesty, and one would not like to imitate the Byzantine historians who were given to similar tricks. One of these gentlemen, Choricius by name, had a seaport to describe. How the actual seaport lay mattered little to Choricius, so long as the Epidamnus of Thucydides was at hand; and if the task of narrating our Peloponnesian war were assigned to the ghost of Choricius, I have no doubt that he would open it with a description of Charleston in terms of Epidamnus. Little matters of topography would not trouble such an one. To the sophist an island is an island, a river a river, a height a height, everywhere. Sphacteria would furnish the model for Morris Island; the Achelous would serve indifferently for Potomac or Mississippi, the Epipolæ for Missionary Ridge, Platæa for Vicksburg, the harbor of Syracuse for Hampton Roads; and Thucydides' description of the naval engagement and the watching crowds would be made available for the fight between Merrimac and Monitor.

The debates in Thucydides would be a quarry for the debates in either Congress, as they had been a quarry for centuries of rhetorical historians. And as for the "winged words," why should they have wings, if not to flit from character to character? A well-known scholar, at a loss for authentic details as to the life of Pindar, fell back on a lot of apophthegms attributed to his hero, and in so doing maintained the strange doctrine that apophthegms were more to be trusted than any other form of tradition. There could not have been a more hopeless thesis. The general who said that he would burn his coat if it knew his plans has figured in all the wars with which I have been contemporary, was a conspicuous character in the Mexican war, and passed from camp to camp in the war between the States. The

Civil War Classic Library

mot, familiar to the classical scholar, was doubtless attributed in his day to that dashing sheik Chedorlaomer, and will be ascribed to both leaders in the final battle of Armageddon. The hank of yarns told about Socrates is pieced out with tabs and tags borrowed from different periods. I have heard, say, in the afternoon, a good story at the expense of a famous American revival preacher which I had read that morning in the Cent Nouvelles Nouvelles, and there is a large stock of anecdotes made to screw on and screw off for the special behoof of college presidents and university professors. Why hold up Choricius to ridicule? He was no worse than others of his guild. It was not Choricius, it was another Byzantine historian who conveyed from Herodotus an unsavory retort, over which the unsuspecting Gibbon chuckles in the dark cellar of his notes, where he keeps so much of his high game. The Greek historian of the Roman Empire, the Roman historian of every date, are no better, and Dionysius of Halicarnassus, who has devoted many pages to the arraignment of Thucydides' style, cribs with the utmost composure from the author he has vilipended. Still, we must not set down every coincidence as borrowing. Thucydides himself insists on the recurrence of the same or similar events in a history of which human nature is a constant factor. "Undo this button" is not necessarily a quotation from King Lear. "There is no way but this" was original with Macaulay, and not stolen from Shakespeare. "Never mind, general, all this has been my fault," are words attributed to General Lee after the battle of Gettysburg. This is very much the language of Gylippus after the failure of his attack on the Athenian lines before Syracuse. How many heroic as well as unheroic natures have had to say "Mea culpa, mea maxima culpa."

[Note: Thuc. 7, 5, 2: [Greek: ouk ephê to hamartêma ekeinôn all' heautou genesthai.]]

Situations may recur, sayings may recur, but no characters come back. Nature always breaks her mould. "I could not help muttering to myself,"

54

says Coleridge in his Biographia Literaria, "when the good pastor this morning told me that Klopstock was the German Milton, 'a very _German_ Milton, indeed!!!'" and Coleridge's italics and three exclamation points may answer for all parallelisms. When historical characters get far enough off it may be possible to imitate Plutarch, but only then. Victor Hugo wrote a passionate protest against the execution of John Brown, in which he compared Virginia hanging John Brown with Washington putting Spartacus to death. What Washington would have done with Spartacus can readily be divined. Those who have stood nearest to Grant and Sherman, to Lee and Jackson, the men, fail to see any strong resemblance to leaders in other wars. Nicias, in the Peloponnesian war, whose name means Winfield, has nothing in common with General Scott, whose plan of putting down the rebellion, the "Anaconda Plan," as it was called, bears some resemblance to the scheme of Demosthenes, the Athenian general, for quelling the Peloponnese. Brasidas was in some respects like Stonewall Jackson, but Brasidas was not a Presbyterian elder, nor Stonewall Jackson a cajoling diplomatist.

IV

This paper is rapidly becoming what life is,--a series of renunciations,--and the reader is by this time sufficiently enlightened as to the reasons why I gave up the ambitious title Two Wars, and substituted A Southerner in the Peloponnesian War. If I were a military man, I might have been tempted to draw some further illustrations from the history of the two struggles, but my short and desultory service in the field does not entitle me to set up as a strategist. I went from my books to the front, and went back from the front to my books, from the Confederate war to the Peloponnesian war, from Lee and Early to Thucydides and Aristophanes. I fancy that I understood my Greek history and my Greek authors better for my experience in the field, but some degree of understanding would have come to me even if I had not stirred from home. For while my home was spared until the month preceding the surrender, every vibration of the great struggle was felt at the foot of the Blue Ridge. We were not too far off to sympathize with the scares at Richmond. There was the Pawnee affair, for instance. Early in the war all Richmond was stirred by the absurd report that the Pawnee was on its way up James River to lay the Confederate capital in ashes, just as all Athens was stirred, in the early part of the Peloponnesian war, by a naval demonstration against the Piræus. The Pawnee war, as it was jocularly called, did not last long. Shot-guns and revolvers, to which the civilian soul naturally resorts in every time of trouble, were soon laid aside, and the only artillery to which the extemporized warriors were exposed was the artillery of jests. Even now survivors of those days recur to the tumultuous excitement of that Pawnee Sunday as among the memorable things of the war, and never without merriment. Perhaps nobody expected serious resistance to be made by the clergymen and the department clerks and the business men who armed themselves for the fray. Home guards were familiar butts on both sides of the line, but home guards have been known to die in battle, and death in battle is supposed to be rather tragic than otherwise. Nor is the tragedy made less tragic by the age of the combatant. The ancients thought a young warrior dead something fair to behold. To Greek poet and Roman poet alike an aged warrior is a pitiable spectacle. No one is likely to forget Virgil's Priam, Tyrtæus' description of an old soldier on the field of battle came up to me more than once, and there is stamped forever on my mind the image of one dying Confederate, "with white hair and hoary beard, breathing out his brave soul in the dust" on the western bank of the fair Shenandoah. Yet a few weeks before, that same old Confederate, as a member of the awkward squad, would have been a legitimate object of ridicule; and so the heroes of the

Pawnee war, the belted knights, or knights who would have been belted could belts have been found for their civic girth, were twitted with their heroism.

[Note: Tyrtæus Fr. 8, 23:

[Greek: êdê leukon echonta karê polion te geneion thymon apopneiont' alkimon en koniê].

The first line is taken from Il. 22, 74. I do not continue the citation because the Homeric passage has not been subjected to the refining process of Mr. MURRAY'S redactors of the Iliad.]

[Note: The Bloody Angle, May 12, 1864, an unforgettable date.]

[Note: Girl in the Carpathians and Scholar in Politics are titles of current publications taken at random to illustrate the personal element and its unfitness.]

But our scares were not confined to scares that came from Richmond. One cavalry raid came up to our very doors, and Custer and his men were repelled by a handful of reserve artillerymen. Our home guard was summoned more than once to defend Rockfish Gap, and I remember one long summer night spent as a mounted picket on the road to Palmyra. Every battle in that "dancing ground of war" brought to the great Charlottesville hospital sad reinforcements of wounded men. Crutch-races between one-legged soldiers were organized, and there were timber-toe quadrilles and one-armed cotillions. Out of the shelter of the Blue Ridge it was easy enough to get into the range of bullets. A semblance of college life was kept up at the University of Virginia. The students were chiefly maimed soldiers and boys under military age; but when things grew hot in front, maimed soldiers would edge nearer to the hell of battle and the boys would rush off to the game of powder and ball. One little band of these college boys chose an odd time for their baptism of fire, and were put into action during the famous fight of "the bloody angle." From the night when word was brought that the Federals had occupied Alexandria to the time when I hobbled into the provost marshal's office at Charlottesville and took the oath of allegiance, the war was part of my life, and it is not altogether surprising that the memories of the Confederacy come back to me whenever I contemplate the history of the Peloponnesian war, which bulks so largely in all Greek studies. And that is all this paper really means. It belongs to the class of inartistic performances of which Aristotle speaks so slightingly. It has no unity except the accidental unity of person. A Southerner in the Peloponnesian War has no more artistic right to be than A Girl in the Carpathians or A Scholar in Politics, and yet it may serve as a document. But what will not serve as a document to the modern historian? The historian is no longer the poor creature described by Aristotle. He is no annalist, no chronicler. He is not dragged along by the mechanical sequence of events. "The master of them that know" did not know everything. He did not know that history was to become as plastic as poetry, as dramatic as a play.

V

[Note: [Greek: akoueis Aischinê]; Dem. 18, 112. My Millwood friend was a scholar of the old times and would not have paused to consider whether the omission of [Greek: ô] was due to scorn of Æschines or dread of the hiatus.]

The war was a good time for the study of the conflict between Athens and Sparta. It was a great time for reading and re-reading classical literature generally, for the South was blockaded against new books as effectively, almost, as Megara was blockaded against garlic and salt. The current literature of those three or four years was a blank to most Confederates. Few books got across the line. A vigorous effort was made to supply our soldiers with Bibles and parts of the Bible, and large consignments ran the blockade. Else little came from abroad, and few books were reprinted in the Confederacy. Of these I recall especially Bulwer's Strange Story; Victor Hugo's Les Misérables, popularly pronounced "Lee's Miserables"; and the historical novels of Louise Mühlbach, known to the Confederate soldier as "Lou Mealbag." All were eagerly read, but Cosette and Fantine and Joseph the Second would not last forever, and we fell back on the old stand-bys. Some of us exhumed neglected treasures, and I remember that I was fooled by Bulwer's commendation of Charron into reading that feebler Montaigne. The Southerner, always conservative in his tastes and no great admirer of American literature, which had become largely alien to him, went back to his English classics, his ancient classics. Old gentlemen past the military age furbished up their Latin and Greek. Some of them had never let their Latin and Greek grow rusty. When I was serving on General Gordon's staff, I met at Millwood, in Clarke County, a Virginian of the old school who declaimed with fiery emphasis, in the original, choice passages of Demosthenes' tirade against Æschines. Not Demosthenes himself could have given more effective utterance to "Hearest thou, Æschines?" I thought of my old friend again not so very long ago, when I read the account that the most brilliant of modern German classicists gives of his encounter with a French schoolmaster at Beauvais in 1870, during the Franco-Prussian war, and of the heated discussion that ensued about the comparative merits of Euripides and Racine. The bookman is not always killed in a man by service in the field. True, Lachmann dropped his Propertius to take up arms for his country, but Reisig annotated his Aristophanes in camp, and everybody knows the story of Courier, the soldier Hellenist. But the tendency of life in the open air is to make the soul imbody and imbrute, and after a while one begins to think scholarship a disease, or, at any rate, a bad habit; and the Scythian nomad, or, if you choose, the Texan cowboy, seems to be the normal, healthy type. You put your Pickering Homer in your kit. It drops out by reason of some sudden change of base, and you do not mourn as you ought to do. The fact is you have not read a line for a month. But when the Confederate volunteer returned, let us say, from Jack's Shop or some such homely locality, and opened his Thucydides, the old charm came back with the studious surroundings, and the familiar first words renewed the spell.

"Thucydides of Athens wrote up the war of the Peloponnesians and Athenians." "The war of the Peloponnesians and Athenians" is a somewhat lumbering way of saying "the Peloponnesian war." But Thucydides never says "the Peloponnesian war." Why not? Perhaps his course in this matter was determined by a spirit of judicial fairness. However that may be, either he employs some phrase like the one cited, or he says "this war" as we say "the war," as if there were no other war on record. "Revolutionary war," "war of 1812," "Seminole war," "Mexican war,"--all these run glibly from our tongues, but we also lumber when we wish to be accurate. The names of wars, like the names of diseases, are generally put off on the party of the other part. We say "French and Indian war" without troubling ourselves to ask what the French and Indians called it, but "Northern war" and "Southern war" were never popular designations. "The war between the States," which a good many Southerners prefer, is both bookish and inexact. "Civil war" is an utter misnomer. It was used and is still used by courteous people, the same people who are careful to say "Federal" and "Confederate." "War of the rebellion," which begs the very question at issue, has become the official designation of the struggle, but has found no acceptance with the vanquished. To this day no Southerner uses it except by way of quotation, as in Rebellion Record, and even in the North it was only by degrees that "reb" replaced "secesh." "Secession" was not a word with which to charm the "old-line Whigs" of the South. They would fight the battles of the secessionists, but they would not bear their name. "The war of secession" is still used a good deal in foreign books, but it has no popular hold. "The war," without any further qualification, served the turn of Thucydides and Aristophanes for the Peloponnesian war. It will serve ours, let it be hoped, for some time to come.

VI

A Confederate commentary on Thucydides, on the scale of the remarks just made on the name of the war, would outrun the lines of this study. Let us pass from Thucydides to the other contemporary chronicler who turns out some sides of the "Doric war" about which Thucydides is silent. The antique Clio gathers up her robe and steps tiptoe over rubbishy details that are the delight of the comic poet and the modern Muse of History. Thucydides, it is true, gives us a minute account of the plague. That was a subject which commended itself to his saturnine spirit, and in his description he deigns to speak of the "stuffy cabooses" into which the country people were crowded when the Lacedæmonians invaded Attica. But when Aristophanes touches the same chapter, he goes into picturesque details about the rookeries and the wine-jars inhabited by the newcomers. Diogenes' jar, commonly misnamed a tub, was no invention, and I have known less comfortable quarters than the hogshead which I occupied for a day or two in one of my outings during the war.

The plague was too serious a matter for even Aristophanes to make fun of, and the annalist of the war between the States will not find any parallel in the chronicles of the South. There was no such epidemic as still shows its livid face in the pages of Thucydides and the verses of Lucretius. True, some diseases of which civic life makes light proved to be veritable scourges in camp. Measles was especially fatal to the country-bred, and for abject misery I have never seen anything like those cases of measles in which nostalgia had supervened. Nostalgia, which we are apt to sneer at as a doctor's name for homesickness, and to class with cachexy and borborygmus, was a power for evil in those days, and some of our finest troops were thinned out by it, notoriously the North Carolinians, whose attachment to the soil of their State was as passionate as that of any Greeks, ancient or modern, Attic or Peloponnesian.

[Note: Gresham's law was anticipated by Aristophanes, Ran. 718, foll.]

But the frightful mortality of the camp does not strike the imagination so forcibly as does the carnage of the battlefield, and no layman cares to analyze hospital reports and compare the medical with the surgical history of the war. Famine, the twin evil of pestilence, is not so easily forgotten, and the dominant note of Aristophanes, hunger, was the dominant note of life in the Confederacy, civil as well as military. The Confederate soldier was often on short rations, but the civilian was not much better off. I do not mean those whose larders were swept by the besom of the invaders. "Not a dust of flour, not an ounce of meat, left in the house," was not an uncommon cry along the line of march; but it was heard elsewhere, and I remember how I raked up examples of European and Asiatic frugality with which to reinforce my editorials and hearten my readers,--the scanty fare of the French peasant, the raw oatmeal of the Scotch stonecutter, the flinty bread of the Swiss mountaineer, the Spaniard's cloves of garlic, the Greek's handful of olives, and the Hindoo's handful of rice. The situation was often gayly accepted. The not infrequent proclamation of fastdays always served as a text for mutual banter, and starvation-parties were the rule, social gatherings at which apples were the chief refreshment. Strange streaks of luxury varied this dead level of scant and plain fare. The stock of fine wines, notably madeiras, for which the South was famous, did not all go to the hospitals. Here and there provident souls had laid in boxes of tea and bags of coffee that carried them through the war, and the chief outlay was for sugar, which rose in price as the war went on, until it almost regained the poetical character it bore in Shakespeare's time. Sugar, tea, and coffee once compassed, the daintiness of old times occasionally came back, and I have been assured by those who brought gold with them that Richmond was a paradise of cheap and good living during the war, just as the United States will be for foreigners when our currency becomes as abundant as it was in the last years of the Confederacy. Gresham's law ought to be called Aristophanes' law. In all matters pertaining to the sphere of civic life, merry Aristophanes is of more value than sombre Thucydides, and if the gospel of peace which he preaches is chiefly a variation on the theme of something to eat, small blame to him. Critics have found fault with the appetite of Odysseus as set forth by Homer. No Confederate soldier will subscribe to the censure, and there are no scenes in Aristophanes that appeal more strongly to the memory of the Southerner, civilian or soldier, than those in which the pinch of war makes itself felt.

Farmers and planters made their moan during the Confederacy, and doubtless they had much to suffer. "Impressment" is not a pleasant word at any time, and the tribute that the countryman had to yield to the defense of the South was ruinous,--the indirect tribute as well as the direct. The farmers of Virginia were much to be pitied. Their homes were filled with refugee kinsfolk; wounded Confederates preferred the private house to the hospital. Hungry soldiers and soldiers who forestalled the hunger of weeks to come, laid siege to larder, smoke-house, spring-house. Pay, often tendered, was hardly ever accepted. The cavalryman was perhaps a trifle less welcome than the infantryman, because of the capacious horse and the depleted corn-bin, but few were turned away. Yet there was the liberal earth, and the farmer did not starve, as did the wretched civilian whose dependence was a salary, which did not advance with the rising tide of the currency. The woes of the war clerks in Richmond and of others are on record, and important contributions have been made to the economical history of the Confederate States. I will not draw on these stores. I will only tell of what I have lived, as demanded by the title of this paper. The income of the professors of the University of Virginia was nominally the same during the war that it was before, but the purchasing power of the currency steadily diminished. If it had not been for a grant of woodland, we should have frozen as well as starved during the last year of the war, when the quest of food had become a serious matter. In our direst straits we had not learned to dispense with household service, and the household servants were never stinted of their rations, though the masters had to content themselves with the most meagre fare. The farmers, generous enough to the soldiers, were not overconsiderate of the non-combatants. Often the only way of procuring our coarse food was by making contracts to be paid after the war in legal currency, and sometimes payment in gold was exacted. The contracts were not always kept, and the unfortunate civilian had to make new contracts at an enhanced price. Before my first campaign in 1861, I had bought a little gold and silver, for use in case of capture, and if it had not been for that precious hoard I might not be writing this sketch. But despite the experience of the airy gentlemen who alighted in Richmond during the war, even gold and silver would not always work wonders. Bacon and corned beef in scant measure were the chief of our diet, and not always easy to procure. I have ridden miles and miles, with silver in my palm, seeking daintier food for the women of my household, but in vain. There was nothing to do except to tighten one's belt, and to write editorials showing up the selfishness of the farming class and prophesying the improvement of the currency.

No wonder, then, that with such an experience a bookish Confederate should turn to the Aristophanic account of the Peloponnesian war with sympathetic interest. The Athenians, it is true, were not blockaded as we were, and the Athenian beaux and belles were not reduced to the straits that every Confederate man, assuredly every Confederate woman, can remember. Our blockade-runners could not supply the demands of our population. We went back to first principles. Thorns were for pins, and dogwood sticks for toothbrushes. Rag-bags were ransacked. Impossible garments were made possible. Miracles of turning were performed, not only in coats, but even in envelopes. Whoso had a dress coat gave it to his womankind in order to make the body of a riding-habit. Dainty feet were shod in home-made foot-gear which one durst not call shoes. Fairy fingers which had been stripped of jewelled rings wore bone circlets carved by idle soldiers. There were no more genuine tears than those which flowed from the eyes of the Southern women resident within the Federal lines when they saw the rig of their kinswomen, at the cessation of hostilities. And all this grotesqueness, all this dilapidation, was shot through by specimens of individual finery, by officers who had brought back resplendent uniforms from beyond seas, by heroines who had engineered themselves and their belongings across the Potomac.

[Note: As is well known, the Greek had a mania for shoes. For women's shoes see Av. Lys. 417. For other cordwainer's wares, _l. c._, 110.]

Of all this the scholar found nothing in the records of the Peloponnesian war. The women of Megara may have suffered, but hardly the Corinthian women; and the Athenian dames and damsels were as particular about their shoes and their other cordwainer's wares as ever. The story that Socrates and his wife had but one upper garment between them is a stock joke, as I have shown elsewhere. "Who first started the notable jest it is impossible, at this distance of time, to discover, just as it is impossible to tell whose refined wit originated the conception of the man who lies abed while his solitary shirt is in the wash." The story was intended to illustrate, not the scarcity of raiment in the Peloponnesian war, but the abundance of philosophy in the Socratic soul. All through that war the women of Athens seem to have had as much finery as was good for them. The pinch was felt at other points, and there the Confederate sympathy was keen.

In The Acharnians of Aristophanes, the hero, Dicæopolis, makes a separate peace on his individual account with the Peloponnesians and drives a brisk trade with the different cantons, the enthusiasm reaching its height when the Boeotian appears with his ducks and his eels. This ecstasy can best be understood by those who have seen the capture of a sutler's wagon by hungry Confederates; and the fantastic vision of a separate peace became a sober reality at many points on the lines of the contending parties. The Federal outposts twitted ours with their lack of coffee and sugar; ours taunted the Federals with their lack of tobacco. Such gibes often led, despite the officers, to friendly interchange. So, for instance, a toy-boat which bore the significant name of a parasite familiar to both sides made regular trips across the Rappahannock after the dire struggle at Fredericksburg, and promoted international exchange between "Yank" and "Johnny Reb." The daydream of Aristophanes became a sober certainty.

The war was not an era of sweetness and light. Perhaps sugar was the article most missed. Maple sugar was of too limited production to meet the popular need. Sorghum was a horror then, is a horror to remember now. It set our teeth on edge and clawed off the coats of our stomachs. In the army sugar was doled out by pinches, and from the tables of most citizens it was banished altogether. There were those who solaced themselves with rye coffee and sorghum molasses regardless of ergot and acid, but nobler souls would not be untrue to their gastronomic ideal. Necessity is one thing, mock luxury another. If there had been honey enough, we should have been on the antique basis; for honey was the sugar of antiquity, and all our cry for sugar was but an echo of the cry for honey in the Peloponnesian war. Honey was then, as it is now, one of the chief products of Attica. It is not likely that the Peloponnesians took the trouble to burn over the beds of thyme that gave Attic honey its peculiar flavor, but the Peloponnesians would not have been soldiers if they had not robbed every beehive on the march; and, sad to relate, the Athenians must have been forced to import honey. When Dicæopolis makes the separate peace mentioned above, he gets up a feast of good things, and there is a certain unction in the tone with which he orders the basting of sausage-meat with honey, as one should say mutton and currant jelly. In The Peace, when War appears and proceeds to make a salad, he says,--

I'll pour some Attic honey in.

Whereupon Trygæus cries out,--

Ho, there, I warn you use some other honey. Be sparing of the Attic. That costs sixpence.

Attic honey has the ring of New Orleans molasses; "those molasses," as the article was often called, with an admiring plural of majesty.

[Note: Almost as touching as the _pluralis maiestaticus_ of "those molasses" is the

Scythian archer's personification of honey as
[Greek: Attikos melis], Ar. Thesm. 1192.]

But a Confederate student, like the rest of his
tribe, could more readily renounce sweetness
than light, and light soon became a serious
matter. The American demands a flood of light,
and wonders at the English don who pursues his
investigations by the glimmer of two candles.
It was hard to go back to primitive tallow
dips. Lard might have served, but it was too
precious to be used in lamps. The new devices
were dismal, such as the vile stuff called
terebene, which smoked and smelt more than it
illuminated, such as the wax tapers which were
coiled round bottles that had seen better days.
Many preferred the old way, and read by
flickering pine-knots, which cost many an old
reader his eyes.

Now, tallow dips, lard, wax tapers, terebene,
pine-knots, were all represented in the
Peloponnesian war by oil. Oil, one of the great
staples of Attica, became scarcer as the war
went on. "A bibulous wick" was a sinner against
domestic economy; to trim a lamp and hasten
combustion was little short of a crime.
Management in the use of oil--otherwise
considered the height of niggardliness--was the
rule, and could be all the more readily
understood by the Confederate student when he
reflected that oil was the great lubricant as
well; that it was the Attic butter, and to a
considerable extent the Attic soap. Under the
Confederacy butter mounted to the financial
milky way, not to be scaled of ordinary men,
and soap was also a problem. Modern chemists
have denied the existence of true soap in
antiquity. The soap-suds that got into the eyes
of the Athenian boy on the occasion of his
Saturday-night scrubbing were not real soap-
suds, but a kind of lye used for desperate
cases. The oil-flask was the Athenian's
soapbox. No wonder, then, that oil was
exceeding precious in the Peloponnesian war,
and no wonder that all these little details of
daily hardship come back even now to the old

student when he reopens his Aristophanes. No
wonder that the ever present Peloponnesian war
will not suffer him to forget those four years
in which the sea of trouble rose higher and
higher.

NOTES

[Transcriber's note: the 'Notes' have been
moved to their respective pages and appear as
'Notes']

POSTSCRIPT.--The bulk of the Notes would
have been greatly   augmented, if I had
undertaken to explain 1892 as well as 1865 to
the children of 1915. In 1892 Mr. CARNEGIE (p.
19) was not yet the   benefactor of the
outworn members of my own profession, and Mr.
CHARLES FRANCIS ADAMS was declaiming against
the College Fetich to   which I have borne a
life long allegiance. To some of my own
allusions I have lost the clue and find myself
in the category with   which BROWNING has
made the world familiar.

CONTEMPORANEOUS OPINIONS OF THE NORTHERN PRESS

"A poetical view of the Southern cause in the
Civil War."--The Nation, January, 1892.

"An attempt on the part of Professor
Gildersleeve to make the Creed of the Old South
seem a little less absurd than it has for
twenty years past."--Springfield Republican.

"Professor B. L. Gildersleeve states the Creed
of the Old South in a way to make every
Northern man respect those who took up arms

like General Lee under the conviction that the State had the first claim upon their allegiance. The writer would have strengthened this sympathy, however, did he show that he had been docile to the stern teacher, experience, and had come to reject the parochial creed of state rights."--Literary World, January 2, 1892.

"I hope it is not improper to add that wherever, in all Christendom, there is hearty appreciation of profound learning allied to conscience and to a refined life, the recent paper of the Johns Hopkins professor of philology will be taken as conclusive proof that good and true and able men could uphold the cause of the Confederacy even in arms, and never doubt in their hearts that they were right."--JACOB DOLSON COX, "Why the Men of '61 Fought for the Union," Atlantic Monthly, March, 1892.

end

Made in the USA
Middletown, DE
04 January 2016